Domestic Violence & Victim Protective Orders In Oklahoma

AF886581

Don't panic!
Call Urbanic.™

Frank A. Urbanic, Esq.

ISBN: 978-1-946481-13-9

Designed and Published by:

Speakeasy Publications

73-03 Bell Blvd, #10
Oakland Gardens, NY 11364
www.SpeakeasyMarketingInc.com
888-225-8594

Disclaimer

This publication is intended to be informational only. No legal advice is being given, and no attorney-client relationship is intended to be created by reading this material. If you are facing legal issues, whether criminal or civil, seek professional legal counsel to get your questions answered. The law cited is current as of August 1, 2017. Laws are subject to change at any time.

The Urbanic Law Firm, PLLC

1141 N Robinson Avenue
Suite 101
Oklahoma City, OK 73103
(405) 633-3420

Frank@Urbanic.Law

www.Urbanic.Law

Table Of Contents

About Frank Urbanic **6**

Definition of Domestic Violence In Oklahoma **10**

Penalties For Domestic Abuse Charges In Oklahoma **13**

- First Offense 13
- Second Or Subsequent Instance 13
- Domestic Abuse Committed In The Presence Of A Child 13
- Domestic Abuse Committed Against A Pregnant Woman 14
- Domestic Abuse Resulting In Great Bodily Injury 14
- Domestic Abuse By Strangulation 15

After A Domestic Abuse Arrest **16**

- Are Domestic Abuse Charges Bondable? 16
- Will Someone Be Prevented From Having Contact With Their Spouse Or Children In A Domestic Abuse Case? 16

Physical Injury In Domestic Abuse Cases **18**

Prior Occurrences Of Domestic Abuse **19**

- Second Instance Is A Felony 19
- What Happens If The Alleged Victim Recants Their Statement In A Domestic Violence Case? 21
- Will Somoene Get Arrested If The Police Are Called To A Domestic Violence Scene? 24

Domestic Abuse Counseling **25**

- Batterer's Intervention Program 25
- I Recommend Pre-Trial Classes For My Clients 26

The Importance Of Hiring An Experienced Attorney To Handle A Domestic Abuse Case **28**

Military & Domestic Violence **31**

What Is A Victim Protective Order (VPO)? **36**

- What A VPO Can't Do 36

Who Can Obtain A VPO **37**

Stalking 38
Harassment 39
Family Members Of A Victim Of First-Degree Murder 40

Restrictions A VPO Has On A Defendant **41**

How To Get A VPO **45**

Emergency Ex-parte Order 45
Emergency Temporary Ex-parte Order 46
VPO Hearing 47
What To Expect At The Hearing 48
What Happens After The Judge Signs A VPO? 51

Preparing For A VPO Hearing **53**

What To Do If Someone Files A VPO On You **56**

Testifying At The VPO Hearing **59**

Duration Of A VPO **60**

Violating A Protective Order **62**

Violation Of VPO That Causes Physical Injury Or Physical Impairment 62

How A VPO Can Get Dropped **64**

Expunging A VPO **65**

Services For Victims Of Domestic Violence **68**

Definitions **69**

About Frank Urbanic

I became a criminal defense attorney because I'm intimately familiar with how precious our constitutional rights are. After my arrest years ago, I realized how close I was to being in a situation that could have negatively impacted my life forever. That experience made me realize how important it is to have someone on your side who feels strongly about protecting your rights.

In the Air Force, I put my life on the line to support and defend the Constitution during combat. Today, I support and defend the Constitution in the courtroom. My legal career began by representing indigent clients. I saw first-hand how important it is for everyone to have legal representation.

Through my extensive business training at The University of Oklahoma and Texas A&M University, I've learned proven business techniques that allow me to operate a lean and efficient law firm. These techniques include document automation, checklists, templates, the use of cutting-edge technology, and continuous process improvement practices.

My firm uses these business techniques to produce high-quality legal representation in a fraction of the time. Less waste means more value to my clients.

While many offices are still dealing with paper folders, we are digital. No missing documents. No messy folders. Using cloud-based technology, I can work on your case from anywhere on the planet. Whether I'm in a Starbucks or in an airplane at 30,000 ft, I'm still able to work on cases.

What Makes My Firm Particularly Suited To Helping You With Defending Your Rights?

- Extensive Experience In Handling Criminal Defense Cases
- Rated Superb On AVVO.com
- Employing Cutting-Edge Technology To The Benefit Of Our Clients
- Providing High-Quality Criminal Defense At A Reasonable Price
- Intensive Criminal Defense Training In The Caprock Regional Public Defender Office

My Firm Has Handled Cases In The Following Areas:

- Criminal Defense
- DUI, DWI, & APC

- Domestic Assault & Battery
- Theft Crimes
- Drug Possession, Distribution, and Trafficking
- Traffic Tickets

Additional Training:

- Standardized Field Sobriety Test (SFST) Instructor
- Standardized Field Sobriety Test (SFST) Practitioner
- Advanced Roadside Impaired Driving Enforcement (ARIDE) Practitioner
- Drug Recognition Expert (DRE) Overview Course graduate

Professional Associations And Memberships

- National Association of Criminal Defense Lawyers
- National College for DUI Defense
- Oklahoma Criminal Defense Lawyers Association
- Oklahoma Bar Association
- Oklahoma County Bar Association
- Canadian County Bar Association
- Oklahoma County Criminal Defense Lawyers Association
- Order of the Coif
- Phi Kappa Phi

Books

- Oklahoma DUI Survival Guide
- Oklahoma Drug Laws

Bar Admissions

- Oklahoma

DEFINITION OF DOMESTIC VIOLENCE IN OKLAHOMA

Oklahoma refers to domestic violence as domestic abuse. It's also sometimes referred to as domestic assault & battery (A&B). It is defined in 22 O.S. § 60.1 as any act of physical harm, or the threat of imminent physical harm which is committed by an adult, emancipated minor, or minor child 13 years of age or older against another adult, emancipated minor or minor child who are family or household members or who are or were in a dating relationship.

Assault, defined in 21 O.S. § 641, is the willful and unlawful attempt or offer with force, coercion, or violence to do corporal harm to another. Battery, defined in 21 O.S. § 642, is any willful and unlawful use of force or violence upon the person of another.

The primary Oklahoma domestic abuse statute is 21 O.S. § 644. It states that someone is guilty of domestic abuse if they commit any assault or battery against:

- a current or former spouse,

- a present spouse of a former spouse,
- a former spouse of a present spouse,
- parents,
- a foster parent,
- a child,
- a person otherwise related by blood or marriage,
- a person with whom the defendant is or was in a dating relationship,
- an individual with whom the defendant has had a child,
- a person who formerly lived in the same household as the defendant, or
- a person living in the same household as the defendant.

Note the wide range of possibilities for an assault and battery to be considered domestic abuse. For example, domestic abuse can be committed against any child—not just someone the abuser is related to. And when it comes to relatives, domestic abuse could occur when committed against any relative—no matter how remote. The possibilities are endless.

Dating relationship, defined in 22 O.S. 60.1, means a courtship or engagement relationship. A casual acquaintance or ordinary fraternization between persons in a business or social context does not constitute a dating relationship.

SOURCES:
22 O.S. § 60.1
21 O.S. § 641
21 O.S. § 642
21 O.S. § 644

Penalties For Domestic Abuse Charges In Oklahoma

Domestic abuse charges can be misdemeanors or felonies. Whether it's a misdemeanor or a felony depends on how many times someone has violated the statute and the presence of any aggravating factors. Aggravating circumstances can make a first-time offense a felony, and they can increase the severity of the punishment for a second or subsequent offense.

First Offense

A first-time domestic abuse case that does not have any aggravating factors will generally be charged as a misdemeanor. Punishment can be up to one year in county jail. The maximum fine is $5,000.

Second Or Subsequent Instance

A second or subsequent instance of domestic abuse is a felony. Punishment can be up to four years in the Department of Corrections. The maximum fine is $5,000.

Domestic Abuse Committed In The Presence Of A Child

Domestic abuse committed in the presence of a child is a

misdemeanor for the first offense. It carries a punishment range of six months to one year in the county jail. The maximum fine is $5,000. A second or a subsequent offense of domestic abuse in the presence of a child is a felony. The punishment range is one to five years in the Department of Corrections. The maximum fine is $7,000.

Domestic Abuse Committed Against A Pregnant Woman

Domestic abuse committed against a pregnant woman with knowledge of the pregnancy is a misdemeanor for the first offense. The second or subsequent offense of domestic abuse against a pregnant woman with knowledge of the pregnancy is a felony and carries up to ten years in the Department of Corrections. Domestic abuse committed against a pregnant woman with knowledge of the pregnancy where a miscarriage or injury occurs to the unborn child carries a minimum of 20 years in the Department of Corrections.

Domestic Abuse Resulting In Great Bodily Injury

Domestic abuse resulting in great bodily injury is a felony that carries a punishment of up to ten years in the Department of Corrections. Great bodily injury means bone fracture, protracted and obvious disfigurement, protracted loss or impairment of the function of a body part, organ or mental faculty, or substantial risk of death.

Domestic Abuse By Strangulation

Domestic abuse committed with the intent to cause great bodily harm by strangulation or attempted strangulation is a felony. The punishment range is one to three years in the Department of Corrections. The maximum fine is $3,000. For a second or subsequent conviction of domestic abuse by strangulation or attempted strangulation, the punishment range is three to ten years in the Department of Corrections with a maximum fine of $20,000. Strangulation means any form of asphyxia; including, but not limited to, asphyxia characterized by closure of the blood vessels or air passages of the neck as a result of external pressure on the neck or the closure of the nostrils or mouth as a result of external pressure on the head.

SOURCES:
21 O.S. § 644
21 O.S. § 646

The first event after a domestic abuse arrest is a trip to jail. The arrestee will be booked, processed, fingerprinted, and photographed. Their bail will initially be set, and they will be afforded the opportunity to call someone for help.

Are Domestic Abuse Charges Bondable?

Domestic abuse charges are generally bondable. Whether you are arrested or not, your bond will typically be initially set at "no bond." You will find out the exact bond amount when you go in front of the judge for arraignment.

There is a 72-hour "cool down" period after someone is arrested for a domestic abuse charges. That means that the arrestee will not be released from jail until 72 hours has passed from the time of arrest.

Will Someone Be Prevented From Having Contact With Their Spouse Or Children In A Domestic Abuse Case?

You will not necessarily be prevented from having contact with your spouse or children after a domestic abuse case. A domestic abuse charge, by itself, does not carry any requirement that the accused not contact the complaining witness (aka the "victim"). However, what happens many times in a domestic abuse situation is that the victim will file a Victim Protective Order (VPO). A VPO is what's used to prevent someone from contacting the victim. If you have a VPO on you, then you need to read the order thoroughly and obey every word of it. Violation of the VPO is a crime.

Something else that can happen is that the Department of Human Services (DHS) can get involved if there was an injury to a child. Domestic abuse can also occur when the victim is a child. If DHS finds out about the abuse, then they may initiate deprived child proceedings. The child could be removed from home due to the violence committed by an individual living in the home and/or a failure to protect by the other parent/relative/other individual living in the household.

Physical Injury In Domestic Abuse Cases

According to 22 O.S. § 60.16, a law enforcement officer may arrest someone without a warrant if that officer has probable cause to believe that the person has committed an act of domestic abuse in the previous 72 hours.

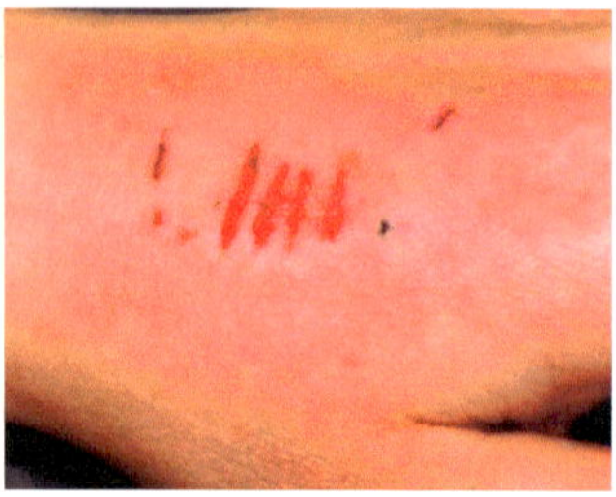

However, the police officer may not arrest a person pursuant to that section without observing a recent physical injury to or an impairment in the physical condition of the alleged victim.

This applies to the criminal part of a domestic abuse situation. However, if you file a victim protective order (VPO), then nobody is looking at the victim to see if there is any evidence of recent physical injury or impairment of physical condition because there are other reasons that someone can file a VPO. It doesn't always have to be a victim of domestic abuse that files a VPO. A parent can file a VPO on behalf of his or her child. Or, the person filing the VPO may be a victim of stalking or harassment.

SOURCE:
[22 O.S. § 60.16]

Prior Occurrences Of Domestic Abuse

The prosecution can introduce prior occurrences of domestic violence as evidence in certain situations. The primary reason to use those prior occurrences would be to enhance a current charge to a more severe charge. On November 1, 2016, a change to 21 O.S. § 644.1 went into effect that makes it easier to charge somebody accused of domestic violence with a felony.

Second Instance Is A Felony

Previously, it took three or more separate instances of domestic assault within one year to be charged with a felony unless the type of violence committed warranted a felony charge. Now, someone with two or more instances of domestic assault can be charged with a felony. There is no requirement that the instances happen within any time period. This is considered a "prior pattern of physical abuse." 21 O.S. § 644.1 defines prior pattern of physical abuse as two or more separate incidences, including the current incident, occurring on different days and each incident relating to an act constituting assault and battery or domestic abuse committed by the defendant against a current or former spouse, a present spouse of a former spouse, parents, a foster parent, a child, a person otherwise related by blood or marriage, a person with whom the defendant is in a dating relationship, an individual with whom the defendant has had a child, a person who formerly lived in the same household as the defendant, a person living in the same household as the defendant, a current intimate partner or former intimate partner, or any combination of such persons.

Proof of each incident prior to the present incident is established merely by the sworn testimony of a third party who was a witness to the alleged physical abuse or by other admissible direct evidence that is independent of the testimony of the victim. It's important to note that the requirement to charge a second "incident" as a felony does not require a previous conviction of domestic abuse or even a prior guilty plea to that crime. However, a guilty plea under any circumstances would certainly also constitute proof of a prior incident.

During trial, a prosecutor cannot introduce previous instances of domestic violence to prove that the defendant committed an act of domestic violence this time. If that evidence is introduced, then it must be for a different reason.

What Happens If The Alleged Victim Recants Their Statement In A Domestic Violence Case?

Victims sometimes change their mind after some time and do not want charges to be pressed on the alleged abuser. Prosecutors generally have a "no dismiss" policy for domestic abuse cases. That means they will not dismiss a case of domestic violence even if the victim tells them that they do not want the defendant to be prosecuted. However, the prosecutor will sometimes dismiss a domestic violence case despite a "no dismiss" policy. There are situations that would make it more or less likely that a prosecutor would dismiss a case. For instance, the least likely situation in which a prosecutor would dismiss a case based only upon the victim's request is where a male defendant and a female victim are in a relationship. This is the typical domestic violence scenario. The thought is that the male abuser is threatening the female victim with more abuse if she doesn't ask for the charges to be dropped.

However, Oklahoma law considers many types of relationships to be sufficient for domestic violence charges when there was a violent act committed between those individuals. For instance, the victim could be a former roommate, an uncle, a cousin, or a brother. Although the prosecutor will still be reluctant to dismiss a case in these instances, the case is more likely to get dismissed than if it were a male/female in a relationship scenario.

A way that charges can get dismissed is when the victim does not show up to testify in court. This happens because the victim is typically the primary witness, and the state needs evidence to be able to convict somebody. If there is no evidence, then the trial or hearing typically cannot be conducted. If the prosecutor continues with the hearing or trial without the victim, then the chances of a conviction typically decrease. However, expecting a dismissal because you think the victim won't show is a risky strategy. First, the witness could show. Second, the trial or hearing could still continue because there is other evidence proving domestic abuse that can be brought in.

Prosecutors frequently continue with the trial or hearing despite the victim not showing up. They do this by getting around hearsay and the confrontation clause. For instance, if a victim talks to a doctor for the purpose of seeking medical care for the injuries they sustain from the domestic violence situation, then what they told the doctor can be admissible even though the victim does not show up. Another way a victim's statement can be entered into evidence without the victim having to appear in court is through a 911 call. That can be considered an excited utterance, which is an exception to hearsay. For instance, if the victim yells on the phone as soon as the 911 operator picks up, "Help, my boyfriend just hit me in the face!", that could be considered an excited utterance, and it would likely be entered into evidence without the presence of a victim. Prosecutors will try to get around the Confrontation Clause by arguing that a statement is non-testimonial. Finally, there could be witnesses to the abuse besides the victim who could testify.

It is important that you don't prevent the victim from showing up at court or encourage them to not testify. That could be considered witness tampering or obstruction of justice, which are crimes. If a witness receives a subpoena to testify in court, they are required to obey the subpoena. Failure to comply with a subpoena could result in being held in contempt of court.

Per 22 O.S. § 720, law enforcement may detain someone whom they have probable cause to believe is a necessary and material witness to a felony if the officer has probable cause to believe that person will refuse to appear in court. However, no person may be detained as a material witness to a crime who is a victim of such crime.

Will Someone Get Arrested If The Police Are Called To A Domestic Violence Scene?

Someone will typically get arrested if the police are called to a domestic violence scene. It's even possible for the person calling the police to get arrested. People think that calling the police will help defuse the situation. It's logical that many people are not familiar with the responsibility of law enforcement and the prosecutor in domestic violence situation. While it's possible that the police can just defuse the situation and nobody will get arrested, that is highly unlikely. Officers are encouraged to arrest someone when a domestic abuse situation is reported.

According to 22 O.S. § 60.16, a law enforcement officer may make a warrantless arrest if the officer has probable cause to believe the person has committed an act of domestic abuse within the preceding 72 hours—even if the assault did not take place in the presence of the officer. An officer may not arrest someone without first observing a recent physical injury to, or an impairment of the physical condition of, the alleged victim.

SOURCES:
22 O.S. § 60.16
21 O.S. § 644.1
22 O.S. § 720

Defendants can take some steps to get a head start on probation requirements and potentially improve the plea deal. These include classes and counseling.

Batterer's Intervention Program

A mandatory condition of a suspended sentence or probation for domestic abuse crimes is that the defendant participates in counseling or undergo treatment for domestic abuse by a counselor. This program is known as the Batterer's Intervention Program (BIP). It's a 52-week course with one session per week. The cost is generally $20 a session. Three unexcused absences in succession or seven unexcused absences in a 52-week period is considered a violation of conditions of probation. If you have too many absences, then you will be kicked out of the class and have to start all over. Failure to attend the classes could result in a conviction, jail, or prison.

In addition to BIP, some counties require that prior to attending BIP, the defendant must undergo either a mental health evaluation or a domestic violence inventory. These evaluations can range from $150 to $250. I get my clients who are charged with domestic abuse into BIP as soon as possible. I provide them a list of locations that offer BIP and the various evaluations.

I Recommend Pre-Trial Classes For My Clients

Completing classes while a case is pending does a couple of things. First, it can often improve the plea recommendation from the prosecutor. We can usually decrease the number of years of incarceration or probation and/or bring it down from a suspended sentence to a deferred sentence. This could be the difference between an automatic conviction and never receiving a conviction. There are also other classes that may be requested by the prosecutor based on the actual situation. An example of this is anger management classes.

There is a misconception that doing classes or going to counseling prior to pleading demonstrates the defendant's guilt. That is absolutely not the case. Most cases end in a negotiated plea. Prosecutors place great value on the classes or counseling a defendant attends. Knocking out some probation requirements prior to a plea almost always improves the plea offer. Sometimes, the facts in a case are so bad that the only way to improve the outcome is to take classes. Delaying or not taking classes will not help a defendant's case. Getting as many classes and other probation requirements quickly completed impresses prosecutors and demonstrates to them that you are taking your situation seriously. If you want to improve the outcome in your case, then you should start the recommended classes and/or counseling as soon as possible.

SOURCE:
21 O.S. § 644

The Importance Of Hiring An Experienced Attorney To Handle A Domestic Abuse Case

Domestic abuse cases can have serious consequences that many people don't realize. The biggest one is the impact on the individual's ability to carry a firearm. A federal law, known as the Lautenberg Amendment, makes it a felony for anyone who is involved in a crime of domestic violence to ship, transport, or receive firearms. This is a federal crime. The bottom line is that the federal government feels that people who have misdemeanor convictions of domestic assault should not possess firearms. The reason the Lautenberg Amendment only applies to misdemeanors is because it's a crime to possess a firearm after any felony conviction.

The federal government considers any guilty plea—even to a deferred sentence—a conviction for purposes of the Lautenberg Amendment. If you don't want to give up your firearms for good, then it's crucial that you don't get an actual conviction on your record. The period that you can't own a firearm during a deferred sentence is the period of probation. So, once you plead guilty to a deferred sentence, you will no longer legally be able to possess a firearm. You'll once again be able to carry a firearm once your deferred sentence is over, the case is dismissed, and it's been expunged.

The lack of ability to possess a firearm can have severe consequences for members of the military. A serviceman can lose his or her job if they plead to even a deferred sentence. This is because every member of the military will have to use a firearm at some point in their career. A commander will not violate federal law, so it is easier to discharge someone who pleads to a job-limiting crime such as domestic abuse.

Furthermore, domestic abuse charges carry a negative stigma that other misdemeanors do not carry. Society views an assault and battery against someone with whom the perpetrator is in a relationship as worse than an assault and battery against an unknown person. Most people do not know that Oklahoma's domestic abuse laws are very broad and cover much more than a spousal battery. And when people hear "domestic violence," an image of a much stronger man wailing on a defenseless woman typically comes to mind. Therefore, it is important to have an attorney who understands the harsh implications of a domestic abuse charge. I am constantly trying to resolve my clients' cases in a way that will have the least negative impact on their lives.

SOURCE:
18 U.S.C. § 922(g)(9)

MILITARY & DOMESTIC VIOLENCE

Getting a domestic violence conviction as a member of the military can end a career. In my 17+ years in the military, I have seen this happen to many people. If you get arrested for domestic violence, your career could effectively be over. You typically won't be allowed to promote or re-enlist.

It's very important that service members have an outcome to the case that doesn't have them pleading guilty to a domestic violence offense. A huge reason for this is because the Lautenberg Amendment, a federal law, prohibits individuals from possessing a firearm if they plead guilty to a misdemeanor domestic violence offense. It is illegal to possess a firearm after pleading guilty to any felony offense. If you can't legally possess a firearm, then it's very difficult to be in the armed services. The ability to use a firearm is crucial for all members of the military. It would be very helpful to get a domestic assault and battery charge for a member of the military reduced to something no worse than "simple" assault and battery. It is not a federal crime for someone to possess a firearm after pleading guilty to just A&B.

An issue that I see with members of the military, having been in active-duty for over ten years, is that members who get arrested are believed to be guilty just because they were arrested. Our system is supposed to presume people innocent until proven guilty. Unfortunately, that's not the case with many military unit commanders. What they'll do is try and make an example out of people.

Take an arrest that happens over the weekend as an example. The commander will find out about it and have the individual report in their service dress uniform early Monday morning. The commander will grill them about what happened. The member may even have to talk to several commanders about what happened. And this isn't just for domestic violence arrests. This happens with any arrest. Additionally, the individual may have to stand before their peers and explain what happened. I've even seen a situation where the commander opened it up to questions from members of the audience. People in the audience were asking the arrestee questions! So, these are all things that members of the military can be subjected to—shame, embarrassment, and railroading.

The biggest problem here is the breakdown in the presumption of innocence. Therefore, I try as hard as I can to get across the importance of maintaining the presumption of innocence. If you go before your commander, then you can exercise your right to remain silent. You don't have to tell people what happened. What you say can and will be held against you—even though it's not to law enforcement. Once you tell one person, it's over. Let your attorney look over the evidence and discuss your case with you before you talk about it with anybody. You'll be threatened and made to feel bad, but just know that you have rights. Don't let higher-ranking people trample on those rights.

If you're in the military and you get arrested, you can be tried on or off base. If it's off base, then it will be handled by the state or city prosecutor. It's usually not transferred to the JAG office on base. However, that does happen sometimes. If you're arrested on base, then it's very likely that your case will be prosecuted on base. The base's Area Defense Counsel helps defend people on base. They're the public defenders for members of the military. You can certainly hire a private attorney to handle your case on base. You would want somebody who's familiar with the UCMJ, the Uniform Code of Military Justice, because that's the body of law that they'll be using to prosecute you.

If you're prosecuted off base, you want representation from someone who's familiar with the procedures and the law for whatever jurisdiction is prosecuting you. Therefore, the Area Defense Counsel will likely not be helping you if your case is prosecuted off base.

Another consequence that arrested members of the military face is an Article 15—known as "non-judicial punishment." Instead of going through a Court Martial, the commander can punish the member through an Article 15. This basically means that the commander can punish the member in some way. Instead of going through a Court Martial, they put pressure on the members to talk and implicate themselves. It's difficult to get out of it at that point.

The Article 15 is often the easiest way for the commander to go. The punishments can range from extra duty on the weekends to being confined to base—or even to getting kicked out. What often happens after a service member's arrest is that the punishment received through an Article 15 is something that makes the service member unpromotable, so they must separate when their time is up. The punishment varies based on the severity of the crime that the member is alleged to have committed.

When a soldier is accused of breaking the law, the Army issues a GOMOR—General Officer Memorandum of Reprimand. This is written by a General Officer reprimanding a soldier for their alleged bad behavior. The GOMOR can become part of the soldier's military files. If it's filed locally, then it will eventually be removed from the soldier's files. A GOMOR filed in the soldier's permanent file will likely stay there forever; this is devastating to a soldier's chances of staying in the Army. It's important for a soldier to do whatever is necessary to prevent the GOMOR from becoming a permanent part of his or her file.

If you had planned on making the military a career, then one argument can end those dreams. So, it's very important to hire an attorney who understands what's going on with the military, the culture there, and what they're going to try to do to you. You must find an attorney who is going to do everything they can to obtain an outcome that's not going to end your career.

WHAT IS A VICTIM PROTECTIVE ORDER (VPO)?

A victim protective order (VPO) in Oklahoma is a civil court order that's designed to stop violent or harassing behavior and protect a victim and victim's family from an abuser. The civil legal protection from a VPO applies to both male and female victims. A VPO is just a court order. A victim must still take steps to protect themselves.

What A VPO Can't Do

The VPO must be served on the defendant before it can be of any help. So, be sure to have an accurate address of the abuser/stalker/harasser when filling out the VPO paperwork. A VPO cannot award custody, mandate a visitation schedule, award financial assistance, award child support, or award property. However, during a VPO hearing, the judge can help facilitate an emergency agreement to stabilize children pending the filing of a divorce and facilitate an agreement for supervised visitations.

WHO CAN OBTAIN A VPO

Who can get a VPO is outlined in 22 O.S. § 60.2. This includes a victim of domestic abuse; a victim of stalking; a victim of harassment; a victim of rape; or any adult or emancipated minor, household member on behalf of any other family member or household member who is a minor or incompetent or any minor aged 16 or 17 years. There has to be a relationship between the two individuals or certain acts need to have occurred. The person filing the VPO is called the Petitioner. The person against whom the VPO is filed is the Defendant.

Jurisdiction must exist. At least one of the following jurisdictional requirements must be met: 1) the petitioner is a resident of the county where the petition is filed, 2) the defendant is a resident of the county where the petition is filed, or 3) the domestic abuse occurred in the county where the petition is filed.

The actions of the defendant must include either 1) causing or attempting to cause physical harm, 2) threatening imminent physical harm, 3) harassment, or 4) stalking. For all but stalking, the two individuals must have a certain relationship. The following qualifies as a "relationship" for these purposes: married, parent & child, persons related by marriage, persons living in the same household, biological parents of the same child, victim of rape, divorced, persons related by blood, present spouse of an ex-spouse, formerly living in same household, or persons in a previous dating relationship. For stalking, the petitioner must have filed the complaint against the defendant with the proper law enforcement agency before filing a petition.

Stalking

22 O.S. § 60.1 defines stalking as the willful, malicious, and repeated following or harassment of a person by an adult, emancipated minor, or minor 13 years or older, in a manner that would cause a reasonable person to feel frightened, intimidated, threatened, harassed, or molested. The stalking must actually cause the person being followed or harassed to feel terrorized, frightened, intimidated, threatened, harassed, or molested. Stalking also means a course of conduct composed of a series of two or more separate acts over a period of time, however short, evidencing a continuity of purpose or unconsented contact with a person that is initiated or continued without the consent of the individual or in disregard of the expressed

desire of the individual that the contact be avoided or discontinued. Unconsented contact or course of conduct includes, but is not limited to:

- following or appearing within the sight of that individual,
- approaching or confronting that individual in a public place or on private property,
- appearing at the workplace or residence of that individual,
- entering onto or remaining on property owned, leased, or occupied by that individual,
- contacting that individual by telephone,
- sending mail or electronic communications to that individual, or
- placing an object on, or delivering an object to, property owned, leased, or occupied by that individual.

Harassment

Harassment is a knowing and willful course or pattern of conduct by a family or household member or an individual who is or has been involved in a dating relationship with the person, directed at a specific person that seriously alarms or annoys the person, and that serves no legitimate purpose. The course of conduct must be such as would cause a reasonable person to suffer substantial emotional distress, and it must actually cause substantial distress to the person. Harassment includes, but is not limited to, harassing or obscene telephone calls and fear of death or bodily injury.

Family Members Of A Victim Of First-Degree Murder

A member of the immediate family of a victim of first-degree murder may seek a VPO against the following people:

1. The person who was charged and subsequently convicted as the principal in the crime of murder in the first degree; or
2. The person who was charged and subsequently convicted of being an accessory to the crime of murder in the first degree.

SOURCES:
22 O.S. § 60.2
22 O.S. § 60.1
22 O.S. § 40.2

RESTRICTIONS A VPO HAS ON A DEFENDANT

A VPO, per se, does not actually prevent somebody from making contact with another person. Criminal penalties for violating a VPO provide an incentive to not violate the VPO.

The VPO may order the defendant to do certain things or take certain measures that would make it more difficult for them to either stalk, injure, or harass the petitioner. For example, 22 O.S. § 60.17 allows the court to order the defendant to use an active real-time 24-hour GPS monitoring device. The court may authorize the victim to monitor the location of the defendant. If the court finds that the defendant has a history that demonstrates an intent to commit violence against the victim, then the court may order the defendant to pay costs and expenses relating to that GPS device and monitoring.

The court will order the defendant to comply with various requirements. The court order may state that the defendant is:

- prohibited from attempting or having any contact

whatsoever with the petitioner through telephone, mail, electronic means, or any other manner at any time or place unless specifically authorized by the court;

- prohibited from injuring, abusing, sexually assaulting, molesting, harassing, stalking, threatening, or otherwise interfering with the protected persons and from attempted use or threatened use of visible force against the protected person that would reasonably be expected to cause bodily injury;
- prohibited from engaging in other conduct that would place the protected persons in a reasonable fear of bodily injury to the protected persons or the protected persons' household, members, or relatives;
- ordered to leave and remain away from a particular residence at a certain time and date and to take no action to change utilities or telephone service;
- ordered to immediately surrender all firearms and other dangerous weapons within their possession or control and any conceal carry license to law enforcement; and/or
- ordered to obtain domestic abuse counseling or treatment.

If the order is served upon the defendant at the residence to be vacated, the court can order law enforcement officers to remain at the residence until the defendant removes necessary clothing and personal effects and leaves the premises. If the order is served upon the defendant at a location other than the residence to be vacated, the court can order law enforcement officers to accompany the defendant to the residence and remain in attendance until the defendant removes necessary clothing or personal effects and leaves the premises. The defendant, in that situation, will be ordered not to go to the residence to remove necessary clothing and personal effects unless law enforcement officers are present. The court can also order law enforcement officers to accompany the petitioner to the current or recent past residence to remove clothing and personal effects and remain in attendance until the petitioner leaves the premises.

If the defendant is a minor, they can be ordered to leave the residence and be immediately placed in the custody of somebody else. In that situation, a preliminary hearing in a juvenile proceeding will be ordered to determine whether further court action would be necessary. The court can modify a visitation order if there is an existing visitation order.

The court can give exclusive care and custody of certain animals to the petitioner. In that case, the defendant will be ordered to have no contact with the animals and will be forbidden from taking, transferring, encumbering, concealing, molesting, attacking, striking, threatening, harming, or otherwise disposing of the animal.

Finally, the court can order other things that the court deems necessary.

SOURCES:
22 O.S. § 60.17
22 O.S. § 60.2
22 O.S. § 60.1

There are two main ways that someone can apply for a VPO—either through an emergency ex-parte order or an emergency temporary ex-parte order. Whichever one the victim uses depends on whether or not the courthouse is open.

Emergency Ex-parte Order

A victim will seek an emergency ex-parte order when the courthouse is open. The emergency ex-parte order is covered in 22 O.S. § 60.3. This is the most common way to get a VPO. The first step is to go to the correct county courthouse and fill out the paperwork for an emergency ex-parte order. It would be in the district court of the county where the petitioner is a resident, where the defendant is a resident, or where the domestic abuse occurred. The petitioner will fill out a form titled "Petition for Protective Order."

Once the petitioner fills out the request for the emergency ex-parte order, the court will hold an ex-parte hearing on the same day the petition is filed if the court finds sufficient grounds to hold such a hearing. The court will issue an emergency ex-parte order if it finds it necessary to prevent the victim from immediate and present danger or domestic abuse, stalking, or harassment. The order will be in effect until after the full hearing has occurred. However, if the defendant does not appear at the hearing after they have been served, then the emergency ex-parte order shall remain in effect until the defendant is served with the permanent order. If the terms of the permanent order are the same as those in the emergency order or are less restrictive, then it's not necessary to serve the defendant with a permanent order.

Emergency Temporary Ex-parte Order

An emergency temporary ex parte order occurs when the court is not open for business and someone is a victim of domestic violence, stalking, harassment, rape, forcible sodomy, a sex offense, kidnapping or assault and battery with a deadly weapon, or member of the immediate family of the victim a first-degree murder. This is covered in 22 O.S. § 40.3. The procedure for this begins with the victim notifying law enforcement of the reason for needing a protective order. The officer will immediately notify a judge, and then the judge will inform the officer of the decision to approve or disapprove the temporary emergency order.

The officer will then inform the victim or member of the immediate family of a victim of first-degree murder whether the judge has approved or disapproved the emergency temporary order. The officer will then notify the person subject to the emergency temporary protection order of the issuance and conditions of the order.

VPO Hearing

The hearing will be scheduled within 14 days of the filing of the petition for a protective order. The court can schedule a full hearing on the petition for protective order within 72 hours when the court issues an emergency ex-parte order suspending child visitation rights due to physical violence or threat of abuse.

A copy of the petition for protective order, notice of hearing, and a copy of any emergency ex-parte order issued by the court must be served upon the defendant to hold a hearing. If service has not been made on the defendant at the time of the hearing, the court shall, at the request of the petitioner, issue a new emergency order reflecting a new hearing date and direct service to be made. Failure to serve the defendant shall not be grounds for dismissal of a petition or an ex-parte order unless the victim requests dismissal or fails to appear for the hearing.

A petition for a protective order will, upon the request of the petitioner, renew every 14 days with a new hearing date assigned until the defendant is served. A petition for a protective order will not expire unless the petitioner fails to appear at the hearing or fails to request a new order. A petitioner may ask the court to dismiss the petition and emergency or final order at any time; however, a protective order can only be dismissed by court order. A final protective order shall be granted or denied within six months of service on the defendant unless all parties agree that a temporary protective order remain in effect; provided, a victim shall have the right to request a final protective order hearing at any time after the passage of six months.

What To Expect At The Hearing

Procedures for a hearing are covered in 22 O.S. § 60.4. At the hearing, each side will have the opportunity to present its case. The petitioner goes first and makes the case to the judge as to why a final protective order should be in place against the defendant. Then, the defendant will have an opportunity to state why there should not be a final protective order in place. Both parties can bring witnesses in to testify, and both parties can bring in other evidence such as screenshots from a telephone, voice recordings, or pictures. Both sides also have an opportunity to cross-examine the other side. The judge will rule for the petitioner if they believe the petitioner has proved by a preponderance of the evidence that a protective order is necessary.

The court may impose any terms in the protective order that the court reasonably believes are necessary to bring about the cessation of domestic abuse, stalking, or harassment. The court will not impose any term and condition that may compromise the safety of the victim. If there is a restraining order in a divorce or separate maintenance action, then the protective order may be dismissed in favor of the restraining order or separate maintenance action.

The court may assess costs and fees to the defendant. However, the court has the authority to waive the costs and fees if the court finds that the defendant does not have the ability to pay those costs and fees. The court may assess attorney fees and costs against the petitioner if it makes specific findings that a petition for a protective order has been filed frivolously and no victim exists.

There is sometimes a pending criminal case against at least one party. This is typically a domestic abuse case. In that situation, the judge will likely keep the emergency order in effect until the criminal case has been disposed of. This is done because what is said in that hearing can be used in the criminal case.

Courts do not issue mutual protective orders. If both parties allege domestic abuse by the other party, then the parties must do so by separate petitions. The court will review each petition separately in an individual or consolidated hearing and grant or deny each petition on its individual merits. If the court finds cause to grant both motions, it will do so by separate orders and with specific findings justifying the issuance of each order. The court may only consolidate a hearing if it makes specific findings that: 1) sufficient evidence exists of domestic abuse, stalking, harassment, or rape against each party; 2) each party acted primarily as aggressors; 3) the defendant filed a petition with the court for a protective order no less than three days, not including weekends or holidays, prior to the first scheduled full hearing on the petition filed by the plaintiff; and 4) the defendant had no less than 48 hours of notice prior to the full hearing on the petition filed by the plaintiff.

The court may allow a plaintiff or victim to be accompanied by a victim support person at court proceedings. A victim support person does not make legal arguments. However, a victim support person who is not a licensed attorney may offer the plaintiff or victim comfort or support and may remain in close proximity to the plaintiff or victim.

Per 22 O.S. 60.4, it is illegal to knowingly and willfully seek a protective order against a spouse or ex-spouse pursuant to the Protection from Domestic Abuse Act for purposes of harassment, undue advantage, intimidation, or limitation of child visitation rights in any divorce proceeding or separation action without justifiable cause. A first offense is a misdemeanor that carries up to one year in the county jail. The maximum fine is $5,000. The second or subsequent conviction is a felony. The punishment can be up to two years in the Department of Corrections with a maximum fine of $10,000.

What Happens After The Judge Signs A VPO?

The defendant is expected to abide by the terms of the VPO. It is a crime to violate a VPO. A final protection order can be in effect for up to five years. According to 22 O.S. § 60.6, at no time under any proceeding may a person protected by a protective order be held to be in violation of that protective order. Only a defendant against whom a protective order has been issued may be held to have violated the order.

SOURCES:

22 O.S. § 60.3

22 O.S. § 40.3

22 O.S. § 60.4

22 O.S. § 60.2

PREPARING FOR A VPO HEARING

The best way to maximize your chances of success at a VPO hearing is to hire an attorney. Some people decide to go through with a VPO hearing without the assistance of counsel. That is a risky move because the other side may have an attorney helping them. An attorney knows the rules of evidence and the most effective ways of questioning witnesses and presenting evidence. Important issues may be overlooked if one tries to go through with a VPO hearing without an attorney.

After you hire an attorney, you will need to help your attorney as much as possible. This involves giving witness information and evidence to your attorney. Witnesses are anybody who saw the abuse, your injuries, the stalking, or the harassment. This can include friends, family members, children, medical professionals, law enforcement officers, or even strangers. Try to take note of people who were around during the incident(s) so you can get their information to your attorney.

Gather evidence to help prove your case. Your testimony will be evidence. Remember that you must testify truthfully because lying while under oath is a crime. Other evidence can include police reports, pictures of injuries, pictures of a disturbed household after a domestic violence incident, 911 call audio, a certified copy of the abuser's criminal record, screenshots, audio recordings of telephone calls, and anything else that you can use to convince the judge that you are in need of a protective order.

Your chances of success increase with the amount of evidence you have. However, evidence other than your testimony is not required. The judge will still listen to you despite your having no other witnesses or evidence. Remember that to win, your evidence must outweigh the other side's evidence. If the only evidence presented is the testimony of the parties, then your testimony must be more credible than that of the opposing side for you to win.

Write down the details of the events of stalking, abuse, or harassment as soon as possible after the event happens. This will help in telling your story to the judge. I prepare questions to ask my clients on direct examination and go over them with my client prior to the hearing. Having the events written down in a client's own words ahead of time helps me prepare those questions and ensure that nothing critical is left out.

Remember to be specific when telling your story. Vague descriptions will not be helpful. Try to describe specifically what was done, when it was done, where on your body a battery occurred, and how many times the incident(s) happened.

There are some other things that you should consider including in the evidence you produce to the judge. Bring up the most recent incident(s) of violence and the worst incident(s) of violence. Let the judge know if the defendant has guns or other weapons. And let the judge know about any threats by the defendant to kill or physically hurt you.

What To Do If Someone Files A VPO On You

Having a VPO filed on you can be an unnerving experience. The amount of evidence required to get approval for an emergency VPO is very low. Therefore, it's very easy to tarnish someone's reputation when very little may have occurred.

A VPO is very public. It will appear on OSCN as soon as it's filed. Anyone in the world can look up your name on OSCN and see that someone is claiming that you have either abused, stalked, or harassed somebody. And, it is difficult to get that information removed once it's on there.

The most important thing to do when you are served with a VPO is to obey the VPO! Violating a VPO is a crime. Next, contact an attorney. It is certainly your right to "go it alone" in a VPO hearing, but the stakes are high. It's not worth your reputation to save a few bucks. The same reasons a petitioner should hire an attorney also apply to the defendant. However, it is even more important that a defendant get an attorney for a VPO hearing. If a petitioner loses a VPO a hearing, it's no big deal. If a defendant loses a VPO hearing, the VPO will be in effect, and many unpleasant things will happen.

Help your attorney by gathering evidence. It will be the same type of evidence the petitioner will have to produce. You will need evidence and witnesses to help prove that you did not commit the acts described in the petition. Maybe there is evidence showing that the petitioner is lying or has a motive to make these accusations. All that will need to be brought out in court. If there is a witness that you need to testify on your behalf in court, your attorney could issue a subpoena, which commands their appearance.

Come to court prepared. Bring your evidence and witnesses. The other side will need an opportunity to review any evidence you present to court prior to the hearing. Look over the petitioner's evidence before he or she presents it in court. Make sure your witnesses know why they are there and what you are going to ask them. They must tell the truth, so impress upon them that they are not to make things up. Dress nice. Looking clean-cut and nicely-dressed goes a long way. The judge will be evaluating every aspect of how you present yourself.

Let your attorney do the talking. Don't attempt to talk to the petitioner in the courthouse before the hearing if you have retained counsel. Your attorney can talk to the petitioner. If petitioner is represented by counsel, then your attorney will talk to that attorney. They may be able to work out something before the hearing. Sometimes, deals are made that could involve the emergency order terminating after a short period of time or terminating after a party takes certain actions. It's even possible to negotiate a dismissal of the petition that day.

TESTIFYING AT THE VPO HEARING

You do not have to testify in court. However, it will greatly benefit your case in the VPO hearing to testify no matter what side you're on.

Testifying in a VPO hearing can put you in a bad spot if you have a pending criminal case that's related to the event for which you are having the VPO hearing. What you say in court can and will be held against you. The opposing party will likely request a court reporter. This is so that your testimony can go on record and be used against you in the criminal proceeding. If you see this happening, then you would likely choose to not testify. So, the court reporter probably will not even get there because the threat of having a court reporter can be enough to prevent a party from testifying.

If you don't testify, then you need other ways of introducing evidence to back up your case. This must be through other witnesses. Those other witnesses must be able to introduce any pictures or other evidence. If you don't have any witnesses and you don't testify, then you will likely lose.

DURATION OF A VPO

22 O.S. § 60.4 outlines the two ways a VPO's duration can be determined. First, a VPO can be in effect for either a fixed period or up to five years unless extended, modified, vacated or rescinded upon motion by either party, or if the court approves any consent agreement entered into by the petitioner and defendant. If the defendant is incarcerated, the protective order will remain in full force and effect during the period of incarceration. The period of incarceration, in any jurisdiction, is not included in the calculation of the five-year time limitation.

Second, a protective order can also be in effect for a continuous period of time upon a specific finding by the court of one of the following:

- the person has a history of violating the orders of any court or government or entity;
- the person has previously been convicted of a violent felony offense;
- the person has a previous felony conviction for stalking; or
- a court order for a final VPO has previously been issued against the person in this state or another state.

The court may take into consideration whether the person has a history of domestic violence or a history of other violent acts. The protective order will remain in effect until modified, vacated, or rescinded upon motion by either party, or if the court approves any consent agreement entered into by the plaintiff or defendant. The court will notify the parties at the time of issuance of the protective order of the duration of the protective order.

If a motion is filed by either party to modify, extend, or vacate a protective order, a hearing will be scheduled and notice given to the parties. At the hearing, the issuing court will take any action that's necessary under the circumstances.

If a child has been removed from the residence of a parent or custodial adult because of domestic abuse committed by the child, the parent or custodial adult may refuse the return of such child to the residence unless, upon further consideration by the court in a juvenile proceeding, it is determined that the child is no longer a threat and should be allowed to return to the residence.

SOURCES:
22 O.S. § 60.6
22 O.S. § 60.4

VIOLATING A PROTECTIVE ORDER

It is a crime to violate a VPO. This is covered in 22 O.S. § 60.6. The first violation is a misdemeanor. Punishment consists of a fine of up to $1,000 and/or up to one year in the county jail. A second offense is a felony. This carries from one to three years in the Department of Corrections and a fine of $2,000 –$10,000.

Violation Of VPO That Causes Physical Injury Or Physical Impairment

A VPO violation resulting in physical injury or physical impairment to the plaintiff or any person mentioned in a protective order is a misdemeanor. The violator can spend 20 days–1 year in jail. The maximum fine is $5,000.

The second or subsequent violation of a protective order that causes physical injury or physical impairment to a plaintiff or any other person named in the protective order is a felony. This carries a penalty of one to five years in the Department of Corrections and a fine ranging from $3,000–$10,000. The defendant also must undergo or participate in a counseling service as necessary to bring about the cessation of domestic abuse, stalking, or harassment.

SOURCE:
22 O.S. § 60.6

How A VPO Can Get Dropped

The petitioner can win at the VPO hearing if they put on enough evidence to make the court believe that a final protective order should be in effect. The defendant can win at the hearing if the petitioner does not put on enough evidence to have the court believe that a protective order should be in effect.

If the parties show up to the hearing and the petitioner states that he or she wants the VPO dropped, then the judge will dismiss the VPO. A VPO can also get dismissed if the petitioner does not show up.

Do not take any action that prevents another party from showing up in court. Don't threaten or a harass witness with the intent to prevent them from testifying. Doing any of these things will hurt your case and potentially subject you to criminal liability.

EXPUNGING A VPO

It's possible to get a VPO expunged in Oklahoma. Expungement means the sealing of VPO court records from public inspection but not from law enforcement agencies, the court, or the district attorney. In a VPO expungement action the Plaintiff is the person or persons who sought the original VPO for cause; the Defendant is the person or persons to whom the VPO was directed.

The eligibility for expungement of a VPO is covered in 22 O.S. § 60.18. People eligible to file a motion for expungement of a VPO must be in one of the following categories:

- an ex-parte order was issued to the plaintiff but later terminated due to dismissal of the petitioner before the full hearing or denial of the petition upon full hearing or failure of the plaintiff to appear for full hearing and at least 90 days have passed since the date for a full hearing;
- the plaintiff filed an application for a VPO and failed to appear for the full hearing and at least 90 days have passed since the date last set by the court for the full hearing including the last date set for any continuance, postponement of rescheduling of the hearing;
- the plaintiff or defendant has had the order vacated and

three years have passed since the order to vacate was entered; or

- the plaintiff or defendant is deceased.

The petition must state whether the defendant in the protective order has been convicted of any violation of the protective order and whether any prosecution or complaint is pending in the state or any other state for a violation or alleged violation of the protective order that is thought to be expunged.

The court may order the court record, or any part of it, to be sealed from public inspection. This will only happen when there is no objection from the other party to the VPO or upon a finding that the harm to the privacy of the person in interest or dangers of unwarranted adverse consequences outweigh the public and safety interests of the parties to the protective order in retaining the records. Any record ordered to be sealed may be obliterated or destroyed at the end of ten years.

Upon the entry of an order to expunge and seal from public inspection a VPO court record, or any part thereof, the subject's official actions are deemed never to have occurred, and the persons in interest and the public may properly reply, upon any inquiry in the matter, that no such action ever occurred and that no such record exists with respect to the persons. Employers, educational institutions, state and local government agencies, officials, and employees can't require in any application, interview, or otherwise, an applicant to disclose any information contained in the protective order or court records. An applicant does not have to, in answer to any question concerning the records, provide information that has been sealed, including any reference to or information concerning the sealed information and can state that no such action has ever occurred. The application can't be denied solely because of the refusal of the applicant to disclose protective order court records information that has been sealed. Law enforcement, the district attorney, or the court can access those records without a court order.

SOURCES:
22 O.S. § 60.6
22 O.S. § 60.18

Services For Victims Of Domestic Violence

There are a variety of websites that provide helpful information for victims of domestic violence. Here are some of the most helpful sites:

Legal Aid OK's Domestic Violence Resources and Links - http://oklaw.org/resource/domestic-violence-resources-and-links

Oklahoma Coalition Against Domestic Violence & Sexual Assault - http://ocadvsa.org/

Oklahoma District Attorneys Council Domestic Violence Assistance -
https://www.ok.gov/dac/Victims/Domestic_Violence_Assistance/index.html

DEFINITIONS

A&B – Assault & Battery

ADSAC – Alcohol and Drug Substance Abuse Course

ARIDE – Advanced Roadside Impaired Driving Enforcement

BIP – Batterer's Intervention Program

DHS – Department of Human Services

DRE – Drug Recognition Expert

GOMOR – General Officer Memorandum of Reprimand

O.S. – Oklahoma Statute

OSCN – Oklahoma State Courts Network (www.oscn.net)

SFST – Standardized Field Sobriety Tests

UCMJ – Uniform Code of Military Justice

VPO – Victim Protective Order

DISCLAIMER

This publication is intended to be informational only. No legal advice is being given, and no attorney-client relationship is intended to be created by reading this material. If you are facing legal issues, whether criminal or civil, seek professional legal counsel to get your questions answered. The law cited is current as of August 1, 2017. Laws are subject to change at any time.

THE URBANIC LAW FIRM, PLLC

1141 N Robinson Avenue
Suite 101
Oklahoma City, OK 73103
(405) 633-3420

Frank@Urbanic.Law

www.Urbanic.Law

Made in the USA
Monee, IL
05 November 2026

67385074R00043